Disney's

GENIE'S ABC

ERIC and SUSAN GOLDBERG

Disney PRESS

NEW YORK

$4

8/2

FIRST EDITION
1 3 5 7 9 10 8 6 4 2

Library of Congress Catalog Card Number: 94-70812
ISBN 0-7868-3010-7

Disney's GENIE'S ABC

A a airplane

Bb bat

Cc car

Ee egg

Ff

frog

G g

genie

Hh hippo

Ii inchworm

Jj jack-in-the-box

Kk kangaroo

Ll

lamp

Mm
mouse

N n noodles

O o ostrich

P p pipe

Qq
question mark

S s   star

Tt tutu

Uu umbrella

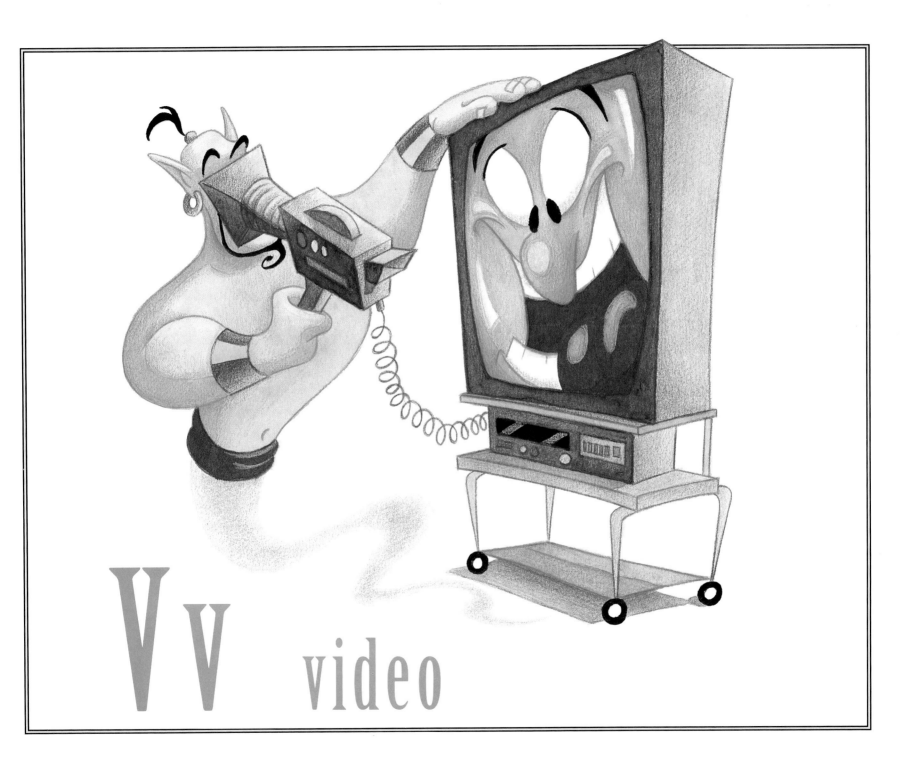

V v video

W w whale

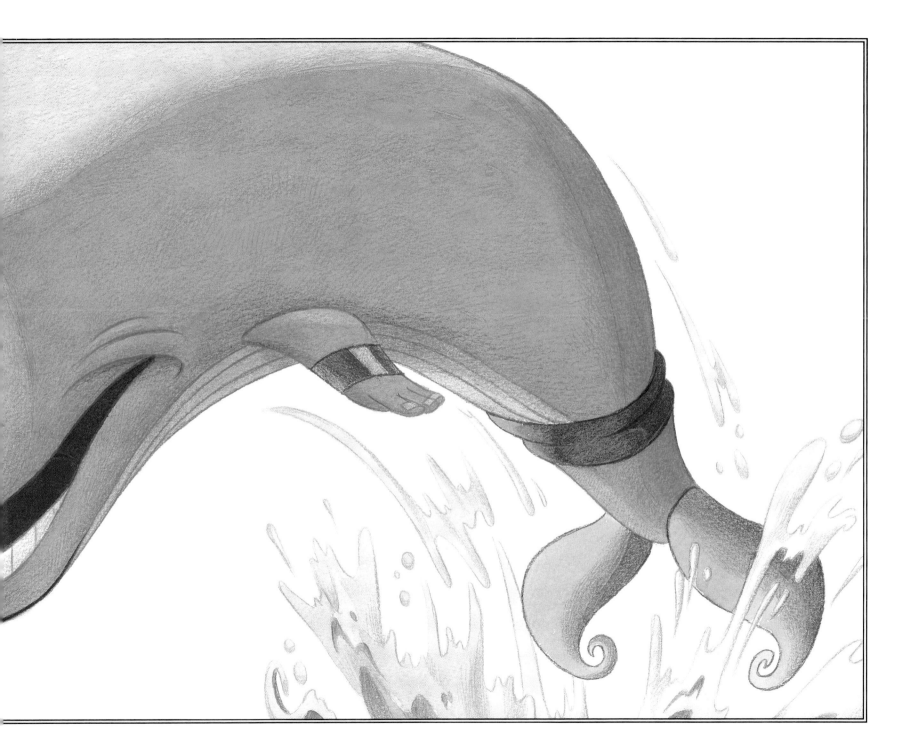

Xx xylophone

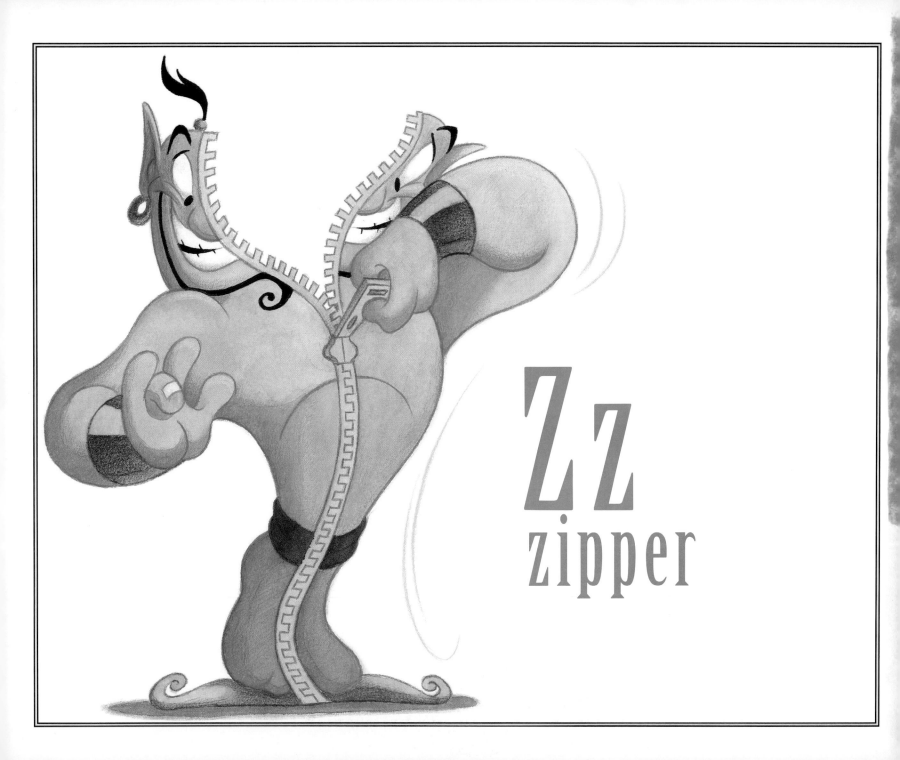

Z z
zipper